The Sun

by Connor Stratton

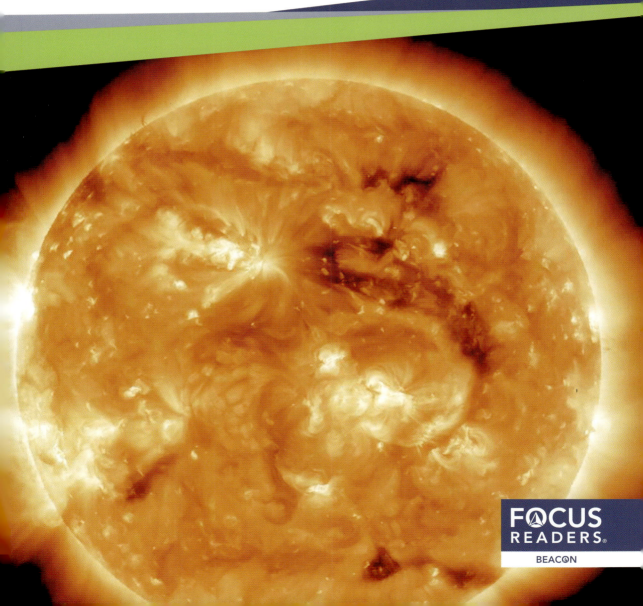

www.focusreaders.com

Copyright © 2023 by Focus Readers®, Lake Elmo, MN 55042. All rights reserved. No part of this book may be reproduced or utilized in any form or by any means without written permission from the publisher.

Focus Readers is distributed by North Star Editions:
sales@northstareditions.com | 888-417-0195

Produced for Focus Readers by Red Line Editorial.

Photographs ©: SDO/AIA/JPL/NASA, cover, 1; Johns Hopkins University Applied Physics Laboratory/NASA, 4; Glenn Benson/KSC/NASA, 6; Goddard/GSFC/NASA, 8, 19, 21, 29; Shutterstock Images, 11, 13, 14–15, 22; JPL-Caltech/NASA, 16; JPL-Caltech/GSFC/NASA, 25; Kim Shiflett/KSC/NASA, 27

Library of Congress Cataloging-in-Publication Data
Library of Congress Cataloging-in-Publication Data is available on the Library of Congress website.

ISBN
978-1-63739-251-5 (hardcover)
978-1-63739-303-1 (paperback)
978-1-63739-405-2 (ebook pdf)
978-1-63739-355-0 (hosted ebook)

Printed in the United States of America
Mankato, MN
082022

About the Author

Connor Stratton writes and edits nonfiction children's books. When he was younger, he wanted to be an astronaut. When he got glasses in middle school, he realized that dream was unlikely. But writing about space turned out to be pretty rewarding, too.

Table of Contents

CHAPTER 1
Touching the Sun 5

CHAPTER 2
Our Star 9

Solar Eclipses 14

CHAPTER 3
Solar Activity 17

CHAPTER 4
Studying the Sun 23

Focus on the Sun • 28
Glossary • 30
To Learn More • 31
Index • 32

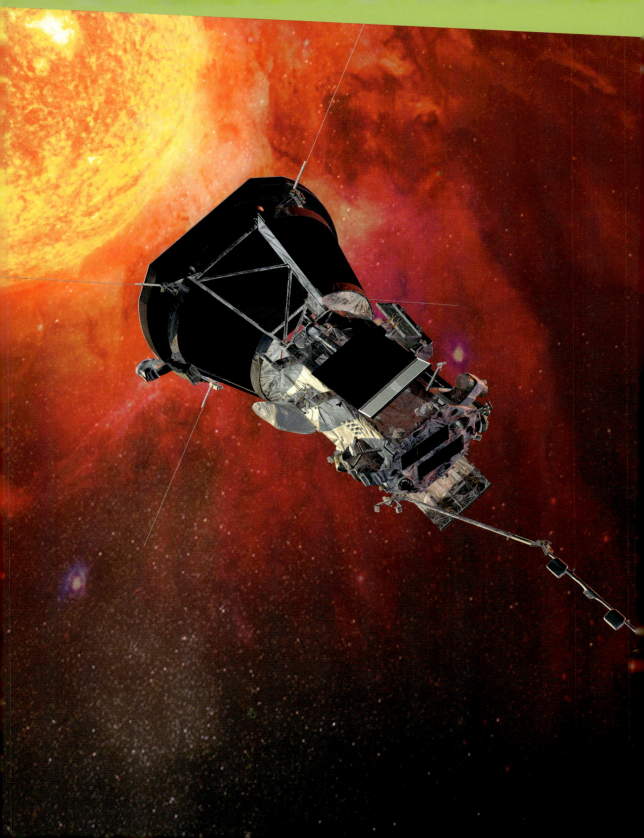

Chapter 1

Touching the Sun

In December 2021, the Sun received a visitor. It was the Parker Solar **Probe**. The spacecraft was flying through the Sun's corona. The corona is the Sun's upper **atmosphere**.

 Scientists expected the probe's mission to last for seven years.

 Scientists spent years working on the Parker Solar Probe.

Passing through the corona was like touching the Sun. In the corona, the Sun's **gravity** is very strong. The Sun's **magnetic fields** are strong, too. These forces control the corona.

The Parker Solar Probe gathered new **data**. Scientists hoped to understand the Sun's mysteries. For example, the Sun is cooler at the surface. But it heats up in the corona. Scientists didn't know why. They hoped the probe could give answers.

Did You Know?

In 2021, the Parker Solar Probe set a new record. It became the fastest spacecraft ever.

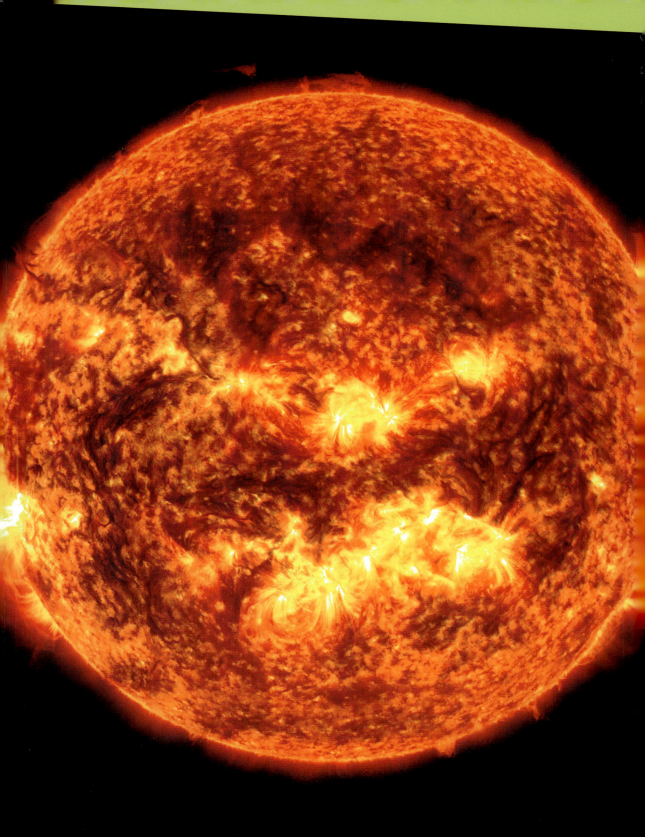

Chapter 2

Our Star

The Sun is a star. It began to form 4.6 billion years ago. At first, it was a huge cloud of gas and dust. The cloud's gravity caused it to cave in on itself. Then the cloud started to spin.

Hydrogen and helium are the two main gases in the Sun.

Over time, the cloud formed a huge ball. That process created the Sun. It also created the planets.

The Sun is massive. So, it has a very strong pull of gravity. That's why Earth orbits the Sun. Everything else in the **solar system** moves around the Sun, too.

Did You Know?

The Sun is an average-sized star. Scientists have found stars 100 times larger than the Sun.

 Approximately 1.3 million Earths could fit inside the Sun.

The Sun is hottest at its center. This part is called the core. The Sun has another layer above the core. In this layer, energy bounces around. In the next layer, energy moves upward. Then the energy reaches the Sun's surface.

The Sun's atmosphere begins at the surface. The atmosphere goes all the way out to the corona. Temperatures change a lot in the atmosphere. But the corona can have temperatures of 3.5 million degrees Fahrenheit (2 million °C).

The Sun's gravity cannot trap this energy. So, the energy escapes. It shoots through space as **solar wind**. Like the Sun, solar wind is plasma. Plasma is similar to gas. But it has an electric charge. For

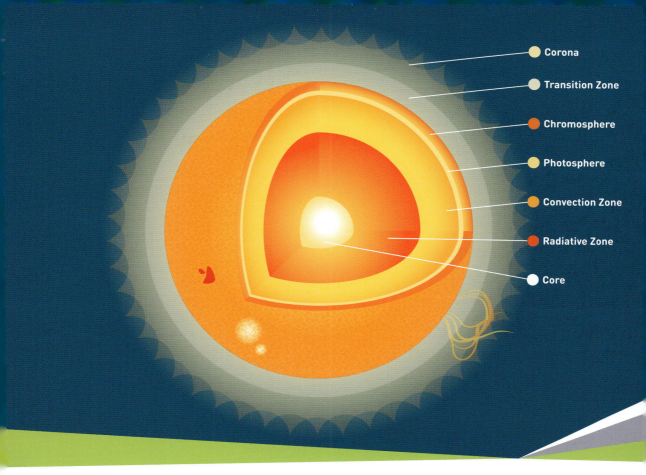

 Temperatures at the Sun's core reach 27 million degrees Fahrenheit (15 million °C).

this reason, solar wind carries the Sun's magnetic field. This field travels throughout the solar system.

THAT'S AMAZING!

Solar Eclipses

Earth, the Moon, and the Sun are always moving. Earth circles the Sun. The Moon circles Earth. Sometimes, the Moon moves between the Sun and Earth. Then, the Moon blocks the Sun's light. A big shadow lands on Earth. This event is known as a solar eclipse.

Sometimes, the Moon blocks only part of the Sun. That is called a partial solar eclipse. Other times, the Moon blocks all sunlight. That is a total solar eclipse. The sky gets dark during the middle of the day. People can see white light around the Moon. That light is the Sun's corona.

It's very important to wear special glasses when viewing an eclipse.

Chapter 3

Solar Activity

The Sun will not last forever. Someday it will run out of energy. That will happen in approximately five billion years. Until then, a lot is happening on the Sun.

Galaxies are made up of billions of stars. Many of those stars are similar to the Sun.

The Sun makes huge amounts of energy and light. This process begins with the gases in the Sun's core. Hydrogen joins together. It forms helium. This makes lots of energy. Then the energy shoots out into space. This energy makes life possible on Earth.

Sometimes, solar activity is fairly calm. Other times, it is very active. During active times, certain events happen more often. For example, sunspots are more common.

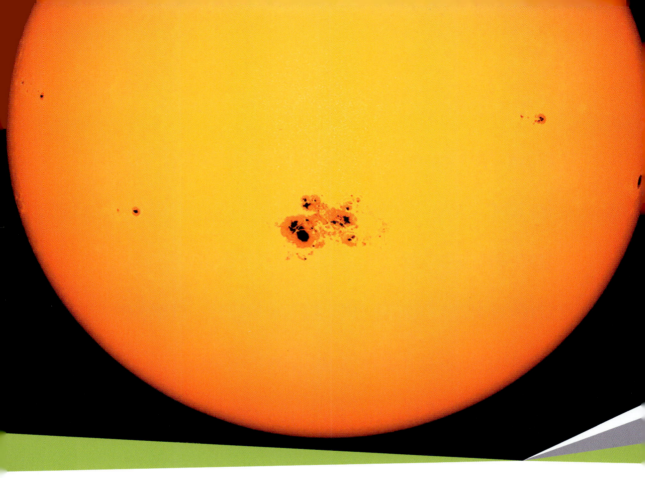

 Sunspots can last for days, weeks, or months.

Sunspots are areas on the Sun's surface. They look darker than the rest of the surface. That's because sunspots are cooler.

Sudden activity often happens near sunspots. Energy can build up in the Sun's magnetic fields. Then the energy explodes. Sometimes there is a huge burst of light. These flashes are called solar flares.

Some of these events can be felt on Earth. They can cause problems

Did You Know?

In 1989, a powerful solar flare took place. Millions of people lost power for several hours.

 Several solar flares can happen every day during active times.

with **satellites**. They can harm other technology, too. Solar activity also causes auroras. These events happen at Earth's poles. They cause the sky to glow.

Chapter 4

Studying the Sun

People have studied the Sun for many years. In fact, ancient scientists saw sunspots. They observed the Sun without tools. But it is very dangerous to look directly at the Sun.

 Ancient people built monuments based on the Sun's position in the sky.

In the 1600s, scientists built the first telescopes. They were able to study the Sun in more detail. In the 1700s, scientists discovered how far the Sun is from Earth.

Scientists made more discoveries about the Sun in the 1800s. Until then, people could only observe

The Sun is approximately 93 million miles (150 million km) from Earth. Light travels that distance in less than nine minutes.

> The Sun gives off X-rays. People cannot see this form of energy with their eyes.

visible light. New tools helped them make new discoveries. Scientists found many other kinds of light. This discovery let people study the Sun in new ways.

Even so, people could only learn so much from Earth. That changed in the mid-1900s. Spacecraft took off into space. In the 1960s, satellites began gathering data on the Sun. Then Skylab launched in the 1970s. Astronauts used it to study the Sun from space.

In the 1990s, scientists sent a spacecraft toward the Sun. It studied the Sun's north and south poles. Solar missions continued into the 2020s.

 The Solar Orbiter blasted into space in 2020.

In 2020, the Solar Orbiter launched. The spacecraft studied the solar wind. It gathered data on the Sun's magnetic fields, too. Scientists hoped to understand more about how they work.

FOCUS ON
The Sun

Write your answers on a separate piece of paper.

1. Write a paragraph explaining the main ideas of Chapter 2.

2. Would you want to be a scientist who studies the Sun? Why or why not?

3. The corona is in which part of the Sun?
    - **A.** the center
    - **B.** the surface
    - **C.** the atmosphere

4. How does the Moon cause a solar eclipse?
    - **A.** The Sun's light hits Earth instead of the Moon.
    - **B.** The Sun's light hits the Moon instead of Earth.
    - **C.** The Sun's light misses both the Moon and Earth.

5. What does **orbits** mean in this book?

*That's why Earth **orbits** the Sun. Everything else in the solar system moves around the Sun, too.*

    A. follows a path around an object because of gravity
    B. pulls an object closer to the center of something
    C. turns an object from a cloud of dust into a star

6. What does **observed** mean in this book?

*They **observed** the Sun without tools. But it is very dangerous to look directly at the Sun.*

    A. studied
    B. built
    C. harmed

Answer key on page 32.

Glossary

atmosphere
The layers of gases that surround a planet, moon, or star.

data
Information collected to study or track something.

gravity
A force that pulls objects toward one another.

magnetic fields
Areas around an object in which a magnetic force can be detected.

probe
A device used to explore.

satellites
Objects or vehicles that orbit a planet or moon, often to collect information.

solar system
The Sun and all the objects that move around it, including planets, moons, asteroids, and comets.

solar wind
Streams of particles sent out by the Sun.

visible light
A form of energy that people can see with their eyes.

To Learn More

BOOKS

Green, Jen. *The Sun and Our Solar System*. North Mankato, MN: Capstone, 2018.

Hirsch, Rebecca E. *Stars and Galaxies in Action (An Augmented Reality Experience)*. Minneapolis: Lerner Publications, 2020.

Huddleston, Emma. *Explore the Sun*. Minneapolis: Abdo Publishing, 2022.

NOTE TO EDUCATORS

Visit **www.focusreaders.com** to find lesson plans, activities, links, and other resources related to this title.

Index

A
atmosphere, 5, 12
auroras, 21

C
core, 11, 18
corona, 5–7, 12, 14

D
dust, 9

E
Earth, 10, 14, 18, 20–21, 24, 26
eclipses, 14

G
gas, 9, 12, 18
gravity, 6, 9–10, 12

M
magnetic fields, 6, 13, 20, 27

P
Parker Solar Probe, 5–7
planets, 10
plasma, 12

S
Skylab, 26
solar flares, 20
solar system, 10, 13
solar wind, 12–13, 27
sunspots, 18–20, 23
surface, 7, 11–12, 19

Answer Key: 1. Answers will vary; **2.** Answers will vary; **3.** C; **4.** B; **5.** A; **6.** A